Saroyani

Snow

Writer's Pocket

First published by Writer's Pocket in 2023

email: publish@writerspocket.com

cover design by Pooja Wadiya

ISBN-13:978-93-6083-797-6

www.writerspocket.com

DEDICATION

I dedicate this book to my all readers and all the people who dream of love.
This book is for all those hopeless romantics too.
This book is also dedicated to all the lovers I have met and all the people I love.
To my supportive family, amazing friends,
This can happen without you guys,
But the person of whom I thought and wrote,
This book is just because of you.

CONTENTS

ACKNOWLEDGMENTS

This book is mainly based on my deepest thoughts throughout high school. So undoubtedly, my biggest supporters were my friends and Bhavana Di.

This book took a lot longer than it should have, in part because it took some deep digging inside myself to manage to get this on paper, in part. After all, the publishing industry is crazy, but mostly because of my laziness.

My cute sister-friends were more enthusiastic about publishing them than I was. This book is as much her work as mine. Thank you, Miss Rabbit and Mahi di. They are ready at any time of the day to hear me spout my poems.

None of this would have been possible without my big sis Mahi di From reading early drafts to telling me how they felt about my work, from being my human grammar check to keeping me sane through it all, they were as important to this book getting done as I was.

Bro, for telling me he loved this book and those lines. Thank you for being there for me, through it all, and truly believing in me. However, am glad to find your help with the editing and analyzing of the poems. You were the first person to read this book, and then, again and again, every time I needed your opinion. Thanks for being there.

Mahi di, for patiently reading and following up with me, even when she got a lot in her own life.

Miss Rabbit (feels weird to call you this) for being my mirror in everything in life your opinion on this (and most things I do) meant more to me than either of us could imagine.

Ram, Miss Rabbit, and him- for being the most amazing friends, blindly believing in my writing, and motivating me all these years, even when I hadn't put a single word on paper.

Ram, for promising to buy this novel, even though I am sure he doesn't read it and we won't have arguments over it.

To Him,

Thanks for helping me find my confidence to be honest you play a major role too in my writing this because if you didn't give me the idea. I would never think of it.

You were my inspiration to write and it was you who made me what I am all these feelings are present in the form of this because of you. You are the biggest reason I started writing. Thank you for being there whenever I need you.

Finally, I'd like to say that this book is for all those whom I've ever shared my poems with. It is my gesture of deep trust.

A big thank you to everyone on the Writer's Pocket team for giving me this unbelievable opportunity. Thanks to Mahek, my skilled editor, and Mohit, my brilliant publishing manager, for making this dream a reality.

Finally, to all the beautiful people in my life. I would like to thank them for being patient with me and for making me the writer that I am today.

I could not have asked for better people to accompany me on this beautiful journey.

A big thank you to everyone who believed in me.

And through these years of ups & downs, I have a lot

of people to thank - who kept telling me they believe in me, even when I lost hope all my online friends even though we are not in contact but this is also a part of my life because of you guys.

1. Dream come true

I am in pain,
Every effort is in vain.
Happiness feels,
like a luxury,
But in your presence,
it's different,
I feel.

With you,
everything's a dream come true,
You're the one who made my dreams accrue.
Raindrops on my skin,
eyes grazing in the starry sky
I am lost in the past,
When we reminisce together,
time recasts.
Moments stretched,
Everything felt like an eternity,
Lost in thought,
yet found serenity.

But when I'm lost in thoughts of you,
Every moment feels like a dream come true.
By your side, my dreams unfold,
You've made them real,
you have made me hold
the hope
In your embrace,
life's colours glow,

your eyes shining with the shimmer
sparkling our dreams and making them true
With you, yes you, my dream come true.

2. On your side

I wish someone to say
Hey, don't worry
there is no need to hurry
if the world keeps us away
and you wish to stay
I will be on your side
With all my might
I don't mind,
I don't care,
because I know
Life has never been fair.
I have already
Decide to be with you
Whether you're wrong or right!

I wish someone to say
if you are in the darkness
I will be your light!
I will try
and
never let you cry
but
if you want to
I will give you my shoulder,
to be your holder.
I will be your tissue
To erase all your issue.
don't worry,
there is no hurry.

when you lose trust in the world,
I will hug you tight and
try my best to make you all right,
I will always be on your side,
I don’t mind,
I don’t care,
because I know
life had never been fair
I will be on your side
Whether you are wrong or right!
With all my might
I will be on your side
On your side.

3. A presence of him

In the depths of my mind,
he resides,
A presence I can't leave behind,
he came into my sky,
Like a falling star,
Memories of him,
they won't say farewell.

In the crowd, I caught his glance,
A moment that left me in a trance,
Sunrises, sunsets, happiness, pain,
With him,
I'd share,
without any gain.
He stays deep in my heart,
A connection that can't
sets us apart.

feeling like this
is hard to explain,
A journey where joy and sorrow reign.

4. We become courageous

When the one you like,
Likes you as well,
That's the finest feeling in the world.

I'm so blessed,
Not to waste this opportunity.
Finally, embrace the courage,
become brave enough
To reveal the secrets of my heart.

I hope
you'll also become Courageous.
maybe the one you like,
Is also secretly admiring you too.

So, seize the moment,
Let your heart speak true,
For love's sweet melody
He is waiting for you.

5. My male vixen

When we first met, my heart leaped,
A connection formed
so effortlessly.
Our souls seemed steeped.
After reuniting, feelings could not hide,
Emotions so pure, hearts open wide.

“I Will Support You,” he said with conviction,
His commitment to her is a selfless prediction.
“I Will Protect You,” his words rang true,
In their bond, trust, and care grew.

Slowly, he realized the depth of his heart,
Her comfort and love,
is a soothing art.
As her gentle guardian,
he'd always stand,
Upholding her self-esteem,
hand in hand.

A selfless man, even when unwell,
he rushes to seek her
in a hurry with worry
They're too strong to conceal,
like ocean waves in motion.

When she was drunk,
he cared without delay,
A man who hides concern but can't stay away.

In sickness and health,
he proved his devotion,
With worry and
a heartfelt emotion.
He rushed to her side without hesitation,
His love was a guiding force,
a tender sensation.

The man who cared
yet tried to conceal,
His feelings for her
His emotions are real.
But the truth in his eyes,
she could see,
He was her caring male vixen,
undoubtedly.

In his presence,
she finds solace and care
A gentle love,
Beyond compare.
A love story blossoming, oh so serene,
Their hearts are entwined in a vibrant scene.
Through the highs and lows,
their bond would mend,
The world's most caring,
gentle male vixen,
Having a
love that won't end.

6. I am who I am

I am the thunder of the rainy night,
A flame that never dims in twilight's light.

I am who I am,
A firework, colours abound,
In the wide expanse of sky and sea,
Everyone seeks strength to infuse,
The strongest bubble that's truly me.

A bubble that won't break,
Resilient and free,
I cherish myself,
unapologetically,
Blooming like a multiflora rose,
you'll see.

In the desert of Loneliness,
I find solace,
I stand tall,
Unashamed, unfiltered, and true,
Blossoming naked,
I won't fall.

No longer masked or hidden,
I am true to my soul's call,
With every storm, unbidden,
I rise and proudly stand tall.

I am who I am, a force to be reckoned

In the storm's embrace, I am beckoned,
Unyielding, unapologetically me,
I'll dance with life, forever free.

I am the thunder of a rainy night,
A flame that never dims from sight,
Burning at the end of the horizon,
A firework of colours, my spirit arose.
I embrace the strength I've found.
I am who I am.
Just Like a multiflora rose in bloom,
Amidst the desert's lonely gloom,
I embrace myself with every stride,
In vulnerability, my soul is wide.

In this journey of self-discovery,
I've learned to love and own,
The vibrant spirit that lies within,
A masterpiece has uniquely grown.

7. Some feelings

Some feelings are shallow, some run deep,
A symphony of emotions, in our hearts they sweep.
Like rivers winding, emotions we keep.
Some make us laugh, others make us weep.
Some we cherish, some we don't
Some we'll want, some we won't.
Grounding emotions keep us steady,
Uplifting ones make us feel ready.
Some we love, hearts intertwined,
Some we don't, like whispers, left behind.
feelings linger, lasting for years
some are fleeting, like raindrop tears.
feelings are long-lasting and true,
Others butterflies, forever anew.
But no matter the feelings that come my way,
Tomorrow brings a new emotional display.
Some grounding, some uplifting,
Some long-lasting, some constantly shifting.
Some we embrace, some we reject,
Some we hold close, and some we deflect.
Some make us smile, while others bring tears,
An ever-changing landscape through the years.
I know tomorrow is only a day away.
No matter what feelings fill my heart today,
you will bring a different array.
So, I embrace each moment, both joy and sorrow,
I find solace in knowing you are on your way.
A brand-new canvas, a fresh display,
For emotions to dance and sway.

Through joy and sorrow, we'll find our way,
As life's symphony continues to play

8. Good byes

Goodbyes can be easy,
and they can shatter a soul,
amidst the pain, the love still shows,
A testament to loving bonds,
In sad eyes, love takes its toll.
Yet in their wake remains the proof,
Of loving bonds that make us whole.
The heart finds solace,
In the memories we hold dear,
Through tears, affection is laid bare,
A testament of hearts that deeply care.
Parting ways, hearts may grieve,
A love that's felt, so hard to leave.

9. Farewell

When parting ways, a piece remains,
A thread connecting hearts,
The proof of love's enduring flame,
In every embrace, it imparts.
Each tear that falls, is a testament,
Of moments cherished, love well spent,
Though goodbyes may hurt, we find,
The love we share forever binds
Amid a parting sigh, emotions intertwine,
A tapestry of memories of yours and mine,
Though farewells may leave us pained,
They reveal unchained love.
We hold our love, though worlds deny,
And in the sadness, strength is found,
A love that stands on solid ground.
In sad eyes, a love-story Told,
Of joy shared and dreams unrolled,
Goodbyes may hurt, but still, we find,
Love's legacy, in hearts, entwine.

10. Snow & water

We both, you and I,
A truth we won't deny,
Together, we can't lie.
We both, intertwined in unity,
You are I, and I am thee.
No lies between,
just honesty,
I am ice, frozen and cold,
You are water, fluid, and bold,
Our destinies, intertwined, unfold.
Our elements merge, hearts align,
In this connection, stars align,
Two souls bound, forever entwined.
Within your depths, I'll find my place,
In liquid love, my soul's embrace.
Ice to water, our union's decree,
A merging of souls, eternally.

11. A story of us

A story can end in infinite ways,
A million paths diverging through days,
lost in a maze,
Now my heart is in a daze,
From all,
you left me,
torn, scars remain,
Love's blindness fades,
and now scars adorn
the hurt refrains.

Days and nights we spent in bliss,
Quicksand beneath my bare feet burns,
Unlike our dance with pointed swords,
Is done.
Love's complexities intertwine and churn,
Leaving me with emotions deeply stirred.
Once danced with swords,
our hearts in sync,
Now divided, lost, a bitter chink.

After losing you,
my love,
My scars linger forever more,
Hate may pass, but indifference is the core,
this cold cruelty, a pain to endeavour,
Mist veils hope and yearning in my eyes,
Still, memories of days and nights arise.

In this landscape of emotions, we tread,
The tapestry of love and pain we weaved,
Infinite endings, as our souls grieved,
Through tangled feelings left unsaid,
Paths diverge, but the pain prevails,
In love and loss, our hearts unveil.
For amidst the pain and memories so bold,
I have to forget a story yet untold.
I'll find the strength to cope,
In the vast expanse of hope's new scope.
A new chapter to begin
as the story end.

12. Sea & shore

the sea and the
shore was born an
inseparable pair,

just like every
couple in the world.

the sea never gets
tired just like
love never ends

they fall in love,
cling to each other,
and get to know each other.

they stay together
for the
rest of their lives.

13. I am hidden & waiting to be found

I can feel myself falling
in hell
life is meaningless
and
nothing is well
I am being hopeless
and
it feels never-ending.

My heart's breaking,
I can feel it shaking.
Now just want to be numb
I don't want to feel.

From late at night
until
the sun shines in the morning,
I am just lying
on bed
and nothing is well
seeing my hope dying
while my heart is still broken.

Didn't sleep last night,
like others,
instead, I was just lying
and
crying under the covers.

Quick, I wipe away all the tears
before anyone comes near Me.
Must hide these feelings from everyone.
because no one will understand
all they can see that
I'm happy and always smiling,
but deep inside my pure soul is dying.

I can feel it rotting;
now it wants to scream,
but I won't
I will not yell
because I know I am in hell.

for the time being
I have to hide it
and
I can never tell anyone how I feel
because no one will understand
no one will believe
no one will ever understand
my emotions and beliefs.

For them to hear that I wish I were dead.
it won't kill them but they'd be filled with dread.

So, I'll try my best not to be selfish.
I'll keep my secret hidden and just let them rest.
because I know that they won't get how I feel
it's better to hide and let them sleep.

14. He never knew

When did my feelings get so deep?
Why did they take that big, long leap?
A leap from friend to crush, emotions steep.
His smile makes me go weak,
His tears, like mine, and,
emotions collide.
From friend to crush,
I don't think he knows about this rush.

His laugh weakens my soul's core,
His tears make mine start to pour.
Why does this happen,
I'm always so strong,
Why does this happen when I'm so strong?
Still, he has no clue.
And I don't think he will know.

I can't help but watch his lips,
move as he speaks,
I'm captivated by his lips,
I can't look away,
Notice their curves as they dip,
it's the shapes my heart seeks
But why am I looking? I don't even know
I wonder if he feels my love's glow.
Does he know?
Or maybe have a clue?
I wonder if he knows my love is true
I can't let it show.

I have to hide
but still, I wonder if he knows.

His eyes, deep and bright, shining stars in his gaze,
Pure emotions flow like rivers in flight,
the heart obeys.
Even God couldn't deliver this much,
Yet he remains unaware of my tender touch.
Though he denies his body's grace,
His beauty could put me in a daze.

His body is perfection, though he denies it,
My head spins with every glance I give,
he could bewitch any girl under his spell,
But I keep my feelings hidden, never to tell.
Because he doesn't know, and I can't set it free.

I love how he looks, who he is,
How he makes me feel like this,
I can't construe
I love his beautiful soul,
But my feelings, hidden, take their toll.
I love his majestic heart,
In his presence, my world becomes art,
He is living every day as if nothing could go wrong,
Yet he hasn't got a clue that my love is true.

School's end comes at noon,
my heart in the gloom,
Does he care that I'm moving away soon?
We part ways,
my heart's soul betrays.

I wish I could have kissed him,
Just once, but I'll keep it in my heart.
But now my chance is gone, I've lost, I'm done.
I don't think he knew, and now he never will.
Now that I've said it, with my words so true,
with this poem, I confess at once,
He never knew,
And now he'll never know.

15. Wish for peace

I stay up the whole night
Thinking while lying on my bed
I am surrounded by
numerous thoughts
and questions in my head
which didn't let me sleep
they have taken all my peace
I think I won't be
ever happy
I won't get a peace
I will never be strong enough
To be at ease.
All these things
keep me up
the whole night
Will this chaos will ever end
Can I get
my peace of mind
before death?
Will I find a place of my own
A place is known as the home
Filled with warmth and love
Everyone is full of care
I don't know if that day will come
On which I didn't hate myself
I didn't criticize myself for being born
Nor do the people around me do.
Will there be a night
when I could sleep peacefully on this bed?

I don't wish to stay up the whole night
I do wish
to sleep
in peace.

16. Byes

Goodbyes may test the strength we hold,
Yet they highlight love's story untold,
In tearful eyes, a connection we find,
A love that endures, forever entwined.
Moments woven like a tapestry,
In each hug, laugh, and cry.
Sad eyes tell stories untold,
With a depth of love to behold,
But in the depths of those teary eyes,
The proof of loving bonds lies.

17. Thought of you

Today sitting with nature
While
Sipping my coffee,
I thought of you again
I pen down my words
While each letter was a person knowing
With how much love I wrote it for you
Wandering through the endless maze of thoughts,
I find myself astray even now and then,
Without you.

So, I write, not for tracing a way out,
My words lack that
But writing you with the thought
that who knows if these pages find him
would he be willing to read my feelings?
Will he read it?
And respond to them?
Who knows what will happen in the upcoming years
What would be his response
I don't know
The only thing I know is
I love him
and it will
increase daily.

Well, Writing gives me peace and
I have a fleeting calm
while my soul is lost in thought of you

And this coffee gets over
with this,
I stop my pen
get lost in your dreams.

18. Look at me

Hey, I know you won't look at me
common
just tell me
what do I have to do to get you
to notice me?
change my looks or the way I walk
change my fashion or the conversation?

My feelings for you run deep,
No one understands why I weep
Except you.
It's true
if only they knew what I have gone through.
the fact that I admit
I am obsessed with your kindness,
But I never meant any harm
If you want, I can repay your
Favor

To you, I remain unnoticed, a hidden rhyme.
but
in my eyes, you always shine.
To you, I am a stranger, nothing more
than a connection you don’t explore.
I will settle with it, though I yearn for more,
fearing rejection,
I close all the doors.

my secret remains tucked away,

pride guarding what my heart wants to say.
I will wait for that day
when I am strong enough to ask
if we can friends
hope you might notice me that day
but if you
didn't I won't cry
I will say goodbye
I will
just cherish that movement you give me
and remain happy.

19. I want

I miss you a lot
But don’t know what to say
Being in a friend zone is in my way
I wish to confess
Without getting depressed if you reject me what would happen to our friend zone?

I want to ask you
I want to make demands on you
I don’t want you to forget me
Ur my love
I wish to get greedy
I want you to be my lover till the end of us
I don’t want it to fade
At least in this decade
I want our love to glow
Just like you
When you said
Let's be friends cutu.

20. Will you?

Will you be my friend?
Even though you know that I love you.
Can we be lovers?
If I say,
I can't be with you
will you be with me?
If I say,
I am not better for you.
Will you be with me?
When I say,
I wish you were worse for me,
So, I don't need to be the worst one.
Will you be by my side
When I say that
Every time you light the hope
It reminds me of darkness.
Will you be with me
If I only cling to you one day
Saying I need you
Will you stay with me
If I become devilish, cold, heartless
Person.
Will you be with me,
If I just forgot to be me
Will you?

21. Love spell

I can't forget you, I'm helpless, it's true,
Though I know I must take you out of my view.
Your memory clings, relentlessly.
Though I know I should let go,
You remain in my heart's undertow.

The way you talk, the way you walk,
Your shining eyes, the way they talk.
I'm still unsure of the reason why,
You're firmly stayed rooted in my mind.

My heart races when you're in sight,
I wish to linger, never say goodbye.
Why you talk to me, I can't understand,
But I cherish the moments, hand in hand.
I can't explain the depth I feel,
A connection that seems surreal.
You talk to me, and I adore you,
Your reactions, the way you explore.
In your presence, my heart is full,
Yet, I'm tangled in emotions' pull.

Looking at you, my mind's awhirl,
A force so strong, I cannot unfurl.
I wish I knew how to break this spell,
But with you, my heart wants to dwell.

I try to forget, to set myself free,
But your presence remains, captivating me.

22. Lovers love

Love is a walk in the rain at night,
Two hands holding, clutching tight;
And everything feels right
Love is honey on a pair of lips,
Dripping onto a heart that skips;
While sweet nectar drips.
He placed,
A tender kiss on honeyed lips
Love is a soft and gentle touch,
A child's hand, a bond to clutch.
In my heart, it means so much;
I wish you hold my hand tight,
In love's embrace, everything's right…
With you in life’s every phase
I am finding solace and grace.
Love is a song staining the air,
Everlasting,
In life and death, always there;
Love, the sun's warmth, the moon's soft glow,
Starry nights, love's tapestry aglow.
Love's light shines, never to die.
Love is a tree with the fruit of sweet kindness, care
love's beauty to share.
With each new shoot, love is
Giving, serving, his every heartbeat.
Love is a document, faithful, strong, and true
Two hearts together,
To one another we forever belong;
In each other's hearts, belonging strong,

A bond that nothing can go wrong.

Love is a river, passion's embrace,
Calming pools, love finds its place.
After the endless fight.
Through the twists and turns, it flows,
Love's eternal journey, it always knows.

In love's embrace, hearts unite,
In every form, it brings delight;
A tapestry is woven with threads of care,
Love's endless beauty is beyond compare.

23. Desires

Desires left untamed and wild,
never to be unveiled;
A golden age of Golden times passed,
etched within our souls,
of an innocent child.
The past and future intertwined,
Moments cherished; love defined.
The child I was, the elder you became;
Leisure days mingled with a deeper purpose.
Felt like time's subtle dance.
Not just leisure, but life's sweet rhyme;
Each day brought a fresh surprise,
Laughter, tears, and heartfelt cries.
Your caring hand, wiping tears away,
As life's river flowed, day by day.
with no stone to halt its course;
Your essence stays strong,
your creed unwavering
In your spirit, strength resides,
Beyond beliefs, love coincides.
None need to say, “I'm here,” for side by side,
We journey on, forever entwined
Nourished with immortal drink,
Awakening truths, I've come to think.
Our love is a feast for,
an immortal source.
A promised land, your heart so pure,
With you, I feel forever secure.
In this vast world, I stand with pride,

Knowing you're forever by my side.
Your psyche free, your creed held high;
The promised land, where blessings reside.

24. Invisible scars

I heard poets are all heartbroken souls,
Their heartbreak seeps,
In words spoken, emotions run deep.
My little mind spills thoughts on every line,
I carefully scribe, my emotions etched
Upon the paper, my soul's outpouring vibe.
A painful shrine, in the dark of night.
Not the best, as you once declared,
Yet my heart detached, my spirit bared, continue to tread, as my tears were shed.
How do I quell these tears that flow,
When memories haunt, refusing to go?
For healing takes time, as heartache implies.
I forgave you sooner than you knew,
You meant the world, but now, no clue.
The song we sang, lingers in the air,
It meant for us two,
But she's the one, now, beside you.
the one to whom you truly care.
she's the one to whom you cling.
Unseen scars, they wound just as deep,
Hidden, but felt, the pain they steep.
They are not easy to find,
Yet, as painful as the ones on the mind.
At times, deeper than those on the skin,
These hidden scars held tight within.
Yet I'll rise, though wounded and sore,
The hidden scars cut, still I'll soar.
A pain in the heart,

no mask can replace.
In this poetic journey of mending the heart,
I find solace in art, a balm for every part.

25. Bound by time and friendship

Through years elapsed, in solitude and grace
I tread,
Countless trials were faced, where dreams were bred.
Tears and errors intertwined,
Yet dreams in heart, forever bind.

Made mistakes, we find our way,
Dreams held close, guiding us each day.
Only by loving deeply and truly,
Do I grasp loneliness and longing's hue?
Only through love can loneliness unfold,
Nostalgia's touch is a story untold.

Only after love's embrace so tight,
Does the ache of solitude take flight?
Dreams and you, etched in my core,
Together we stride, forevermore.

With dreams aglow and you in my heart,
Through life's journey, never apart.
As friends, we'll face life's grace,
Cherishing each day's fleeting embrace.
A single word, a lifetime's pledge,
Sealed with wine, on destiny's edge.

Companions united, no matter how far apart.
A single word, an entire lifetime's worth,
Moments gone won't return.
Sealed with a cup of memories,

heaven and earth.

Loneliness banished, hand in hand,
A simple word, a magical command.
when we unite,
darkness takes flight.

Together, forward, we'll always move,
Through life's challenges, we'll prove and prove.
In pain or joy, no matter the weather,
Side by side, we'll forge ahead, together.

26. Guiding light of everlasting love

I think about you all the time.
You're always in my head.
Each text, each word you've said,
In my heart, forever spread.
I reread every text you send
And remember what you said.

Through every hour, day or night,
I'm here for you, shining bright.
always by your side,
A steadfast presence, a constant guide.
With every breath that I take,
For you, there's no mistake.
Promising to shield you from any harm,
In my embrace, you're safe from the storm.

Love, a force beyond compares,
In your gaze, I find my air.
You're the air that fills my lungs,
In your gaze
my heart becomes young.
I love you more than anything.
My love for you, a blazing flame,
More than words can ever name.

My sunshine on a cloudy sky,
In your love, I'll forever fly.
That's one thing that you are,
A star that sparkles with radiant grace,

In your love's glow, I find my place.
Even in the darkest night,
You're my star, shining bright

27. Is this love what is this

I don't want to keep feeling this way,
You draw close, then drift away.
I seem to be desperate or clingy.
Which I refuse to portray,
Catch me, won't you, before I sway.
I can't keep feeling this way.

Tired of being trapped in the game of flirt,
Yearning for more, yet fearing the hurt,
Once I thought I knew you from the start,
Now you've tangled my feelings, pulled them apart.
I feel pathetic when you mess with my heart.
My heart aches, torn apart.

You're the sun on a good day, stormy night's dread,
Just another crush that leads me to fright.
Leading me to emotions
I've often misread,
A trap I can't escape, no matter how hard I try,
As you tease and toy, my heart wonders why.
I wish to ask you
What are you to make of me once my heart is destroyed?
What will you see once I shatter like dreams?

You're a puzzle piece in my heart's design,
the piece, I can't seem to avoid,
A risk I take, knowing you might decline.
Once my heart's shattered, love's path is destroyed.
I wish to ask you

In this dance of emotions, can we be redeployed?
What's left of me when my heart is destroyed?
A heartache that lingers, a bittersweet ploy.

28. Friendship or more

Are we really
just friends,
mere acquaintances?
I asked,
Just friends, mere happenstance?
Merely companion,
and nothing masked?
Innocent camaraderie that never bends?
Don't look with eyes that linger,
that connect,
so intense and deep
Just friends, no feelings to intersect.
but we still have
converse with such interest,
secrets to keep.

Don't talk with sparks of interest flare,
Just friends, no whispers in the air.
Don't linger in wait for that time,
Don't teach each other, so sublime,
Don't wait,
seconds stretched into hours,
Just friends, no blossoming of love's flowers.
But feelings emerge,
like butterflies,
they throng,
Tying shoelaces,
connections are so strong.

Are we simply friends who chat,
Or is there more to our connection than that?
In every word and each reply,
I sense an undercurrent I can't deny.

29. Friendship's hidden depths

Do friends truly wait so long,
Patiently listening to each other's song?
A lingering presence, time extends,
More than just friendship it suspends.

Just friends like us
Don't teach each other life's simple ties,
Just friends, no emotions that surprise.
Don't butterfly dance within our core,
Just friends, nothing more, nothing more.

Can friends make hearts race
with their just gaze?
occupy our thoughts day and night,
We think of each other till the morning light.
Can friends
Igniting feelings that feel so, right?
Can friendship leave you in this daze?

Friends don't teach to tie shoelaces,
it's true,
But I find myself drawn to teaching you.
In your presence, butterflies take flight,
A feeling that's more than pure delight.

Don't thoughts linger in each passing time,
Just friends, no heart's rhythm in rhyme.
Yet think once more, let possibilities bend,
Maybe, just maybe, more than friends.

Let's contemplate this path we tread,
A connection that might be more widespread.
Could it be that within this trend,
We'll discover something more than just friends.

Question it again, let contemplation bend,
Possibility whispers, “More than just friends,”
In the unspoken moments, perhaps we'll see,
Friendship evolving into what's meant to be

30. Breaking love's chains

When have I felt my weakest,
he asks.
When over someone, I wished to cast,
the weight of moving on seems a daunting task,
Wanting to sever the ties that bind,
knowing escape is hard to find.
From sleepless nights to endless tears,
Drowning in sorrow, overwhelmed by fears.
Yet, breaking free, I couldn't seem to,
Chained to memories, dreams that once were true.

Sleepless nights turned rain into rivers of tears,
Drowning in sorrow, a sea of fears,
Longing to escape from love's cruel bind,
Yet every thought, like an anchor, I find.
Struggling against waves of memories,
Lost in a sea of emotional treasuries.

You yearn to forget, to erase what's been,
To wash away the pain, to cleanse the scene,
His laughter echoes through the corridors,
His touch leaves traces,
lingering indoors,
But every crevice of your mind is a hall,
Filled with memories you can't uninstall.
I yearn to forget, to erase every trace,
Of a love that left an indelible space,
But corners of the mind are stained,
With his laughter, his touch, deeply ingrained

31. Healing love's echoes

I wish to break free, to mend my heart,
To let go of the past, to restart,
But every corner of my being is entwined,
A reminder of the love that once was so kind.

Now, his warmth and scent linger like a ghost,
Haunting my thoughts, a constant host,
In the quest to mend a heart that's torn,
Longing to heal, reborn.

His laughter echoes are now a haunting tune,
His touch lingers,
like a distant moon,
His warmth, a memory I can't let go of,
His scent, a fragrance of love's echo.

32. Is it too much?

I want a place
I can call home,
where I'm embraced with open arms.
A place filled with love
and care
Is it too much?
Am I asking too much?
I crave a gentle pat on the back
and
a warm smile,
free from worry
and apprehension.
I long to shed my tears
with fears
While forgetting
and
leaving behind
the feeling of being an outsider.
Loneliness is not what I seek;
instead,
I want love,
to both give and receive.
I don't want to face the world alone,
I am yearning for a connection
With protection.
Can't I ask for a bit of love and care?
Is that too much?
Am I asking too much?
Is it too much?

I seek affection
and
a touch of protection.
I yearn for the comforting
warmth of love,
not the
frigid stares of disgust.
I want a home,
not just a house.
I want a place
where compassion replaces pity.
I desire a hug that
doesn't make people turn away from me.
It's not too much to ask for, is it?
Because
I don't want to ask too much
Is it too much?
Am I asking too much?
I long for a home that embraces me,
a hug that reassures me,
a little bit of care,
a little bit of love.
A pat on the back and a smile on the face,
untainted by worry and hesitation.
Can't I ask for these simple pleasures
without feeling like I've asked for too much?
Is it too much?
Am I asking too much?
Is it too much

33. Whispers of love beyond

Always in my thoughts, both day and night,
Guiding light, your presence is so bright.
The ones who leave, their hearts so pure,
they don't intend,
To see their loved ones in sorrow bend
Don't wish for pain,
their love will endure.

Those who depart, don't wish for pain,
Though loss brings tears like drops of rain.
Love lingers on, an enduring ember,
In memories we hold, they still remember.
it hurts a lot to part and let go,
But love's legacy is a comfort to know.
If their absence aches with every breath,
They hope for your happiness beyond death.

Thoughts of you, like an unending, steady, flowing stream,
A cherished memory, like a precious dream.
Each word you speak, each text you send,
forever blend.
you'll never end.

In my thoughts,
Your presence lingers,
like a gentle breeze,
In the rustling leaves, in the whispering trees.
Though miles apart, your spirit remains,

Echoes of laughter, love's gentle reins.
Though you've left this world, my dear,
Your spirit lives on,
always near.

From beyond, where stars embrace the blue,
Those who've left, they're watching too.
Like stars that grace the midnight sky,
Your memory shines, never to die.
In every moment, you remain,
A radiant echo, a love that sustains.

ABOUT THE AUTHOR

Snow is a young girl who is currently studying she is from, Uttarakhand, who discovered her hobby of writing after meeting a great friend. She is a writer by night and one of the biggest overthinkers. She started her journey with her diary writing Her work has been previously published in Beneath the Stars, an anthology by Writer's Pocket. Apart from writing and poetry, she finds her escape in dance and music, she is a lover of naps and reads novels, manga, and Manhua every time sitting on the couch while watching the rain, The more people know about her the less it seems she is a lover of romantic mystery. She has now published her first book, SAROYANI.

Writer's Pocket

Writer's Pocket is a publication house established in 2016. We began with the aim of providing a better publishing platform for aspiring writers and budding poets.

The publishing industry in India (and around the world, to a great extent) is always something of a mystery even to the writers themselves. We are working on making publishing more accessible to everyone.

So far, we have helped over 3,000 writers turn their dreams into reality by publishing the books and continue to do so. By doing so, we also provide some of the best content by Indian writers to the readers.

Want to read more books? Scan this QR code with your smartphone and check out all our books on Amazon.